100 1

A *to* Z

✦

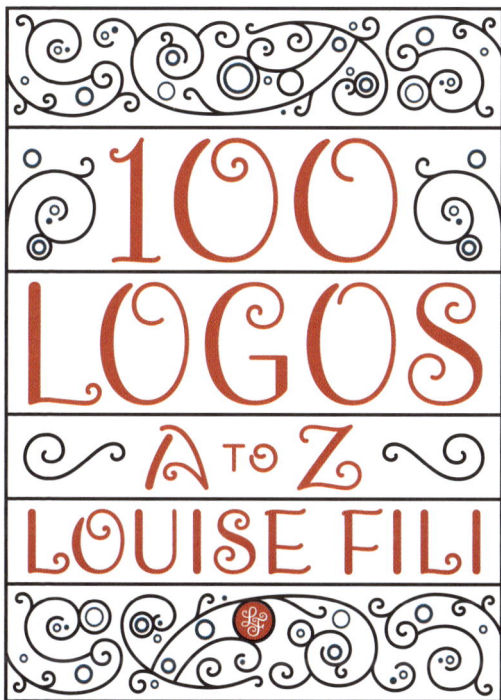

100 LOGOS

A to Z

LOUISE FILI

PA PRESS

PRINCETON ARCHITECTURAL PRESS · NEW YORK

Published by Princeton Architectural Press A division of Chronicle Books LLC 70 West 36th Street New York, NY 10018 www.papress.com © 2025 Louise Fili Ltd All rights reserved. Printed and bound in China 28 27 26 25 4 3 2 1 First edition No part of this book may be used or reproduced in any manner without written permission from the publisher, except in the context of reviews. Every reasonable attempt has been made to identify owners of copyright. Errors or omissions will be corrected in subsequent editions. Editor: Jennifer N. Thompson

Designers: Louise Fili and Christian Adamsky, Louise Fili Ltd Library of Congress Cataloging-in-Publication Data Names: Fili, Louise, author. Title: 100 logos: A to Z / Louise Fili. Other titles: One hundred logos Description: New York: Princeton Architectural Press, [2025] | Summary: "A collection of graphic designer Louise Fili's logos for every letter in the alphabet"—Provided by publisher. Identifiers: LCCN 2024046936 | ISBN 9781797236087 (paperback) | ISBN 9781797236094 (ebook) Subjects: LCSH: Fili, Louise—Themes, motives. | Logos (Symbols) | Graphic design (Typography) | Lettering. | Alphabet books lcgft Classification: LCC NC999.4.F55 A4 2025 | DDC 744.6/3—dc23/eng/20241214 LC record available at https://lccn.loc.gov/2024046936

IT OCCURRED TO ME ONE DAY IN 1997 THAT I HAD DESIGNED A LOGO FOR ALMOST EVERY LETTER OF THE ALPHABET—FROM restaurant Artisanal to fashion designer Zelda. Had it not been for Zelda, I don't imagine that I ever would have thought about it. Thus began a series of limited edition promotional books, printed in letterpress, each one taking me closer to my goal of a complete alphabet of logos. By the third volume, I was unapologetically offering a discount to anyone with a new business starting with the letters Q or Y. One new client was thoughtful enough to name his company Q.bel based on my needs. And when Yes We Can, a chef's collective organized just after the 2008 election, asked for an identity, I jumped at the chance. Once I finished my one hundredth logo, I had reached my objective. And now I can start thinking about the next volume.

LOUISE FILI
New York ✦ 2024

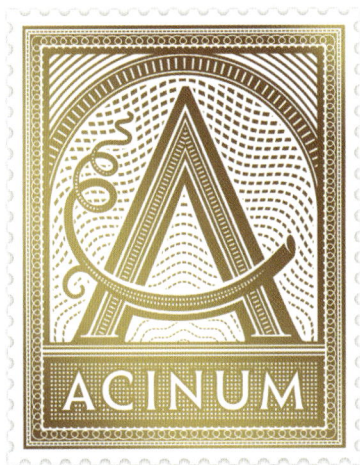

Acinum is a collection of carefully curated wines from leading Italian territories and wineries. The foil-stamped monogram references the delicate tendrils of a grapevine.

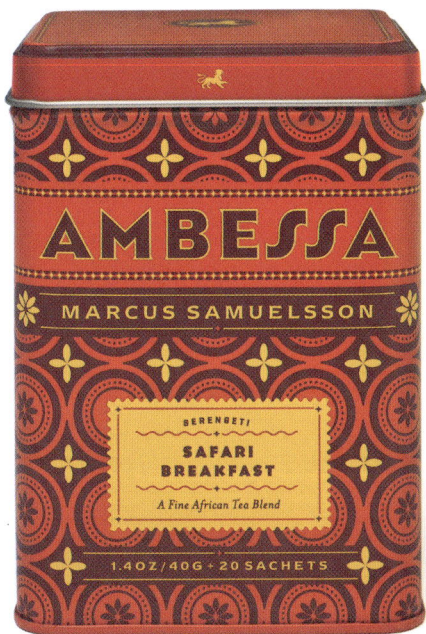

Ambessa (Amharic for lion) is a line of imported teas, which, through use of color and pattern, traces chef Marcus Samuelsson's personal journey from Ethiopia to Sweden to New York.

AMERICAN SPOON

ESTABLISHED 1982

NO 03 ✦ 2006

A family business in northern Michigan enjoys a unique
relationship with each of their fruit growers. This human
interaction is conveyed in the logo's wood engraving.

ARTISANAL

FROMAGERIE · BISTRO · WINE BAR
2 PARK AVENUE NEW YORK, NEW YORK 10016

Nº 04 ✦ 1997

The logo for this New York bistro and fromagerie
is rendered in the style of a classic French cheese
label, employing a commissioned wood engraving.

Located on the historic Post Road in serene Bedford, New York, this is a lovingly restored café, restaurant, and inn. The postage-stamp logo features a portrait of the owner's grandfather.

BELLA CUCINA

Artful Food

The packaging for the Mediterranean-accented, handmade products of Bella Cucina is rooted in the 19th century. Hand-colored engravings and delicate typography create an artisanal look.

Bella Figura

Nº 07 ✦ 2015

An upstate New York printer specializing in unique wedding invitations, Bella Figura uses vintage presses and beautiful paper stocks to produce memorable letterpressed cards.

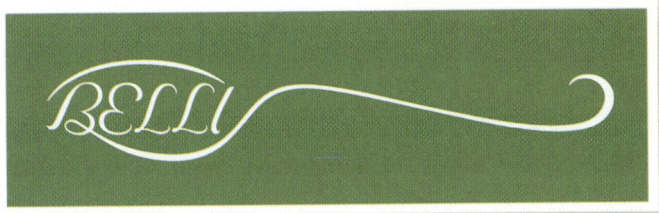

This logo for the aptly named husband-and-wife chef team
of Roberto and Monica Bellissimo captures the very personal
quality of their private dining and special events services.

Bettina is a Santa Barbara eatery serving
naturally leavened, Neapolitan-style pizza
made with seasonal California ingredients.

biella

COLLEZIONE LUXE

Nº 10 ✦ 1998

Named after a town in northern Italy,
Biella imports fine hosiery, and is
distinguished by its woven labels.

BIG ISLAND BEES

HAWAIIAN APIARIES

Nº 11 ✦ 2006

Organic honey from Hawaii's Big Island influenced a
new design genre, "tropical botanical," with commissioned
illustrations of rare blossoms combined with hand lettering.

BLOUNT PARK

No 12 ◆ 1999

A cultural park in Alabama, Blount features a Shakespearean
theater landscaped with fences made from rustic twisted
branches, which served as a point of departure for this logotype.

The chunky, two-tone typography of 1930s Spain
impacted this type treatment, while the color palette
was drawn from paintings selected for the restaurant.

Bonnie's Jams

REMEMBERING *the* TASTE *of* FRUIT

Peach Ginger

*A zesty taste that's delicious
with cheese*

ingredients: RIPE PEACHES, SUGAR,
CANDIED GINGER, *and* LEMON JUICE

Net Wt 8.75 oz (248 g)   9805

Nº 14 ✦ 2011

The labels for Bonnie's Jams—specialists in handmade
jams, jellies, and preserves—were designed after looking
at alphabets and handwriting samples from the 1940s.

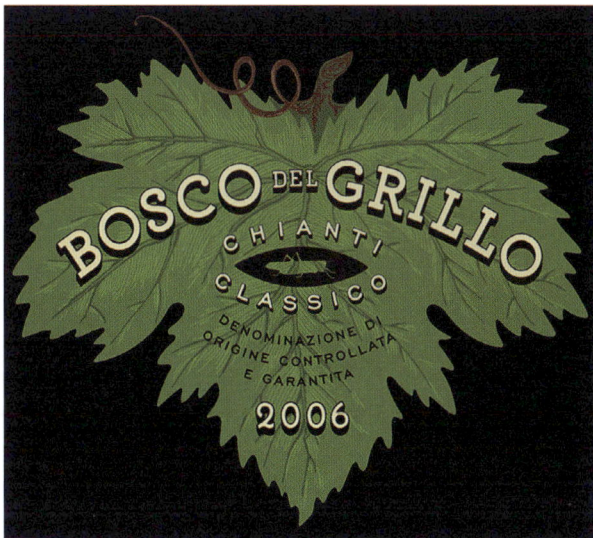

№ 15 ✦ 2008

Bosco del Grillo provided the long-awaited opportunity
to create a design referencing early 19th-century die-cut
French and Italian labels in the shape of a grape leaf.

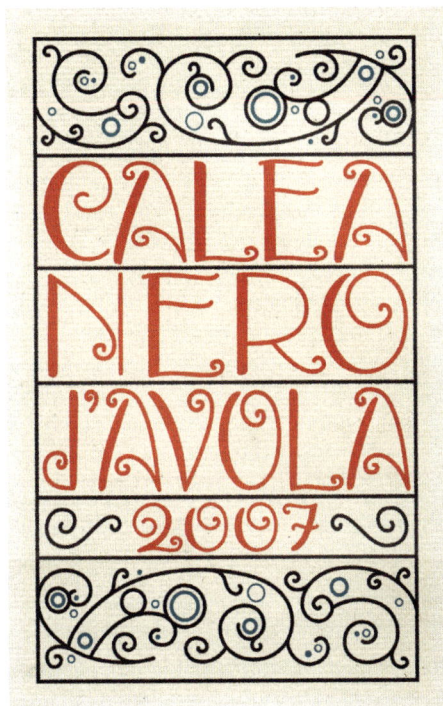

CALEA NERO D'AVOLA 2007

Calea Nero d'Avola, a red Sicilian wine from Polaner Selections, called for study of the exuberant typographic poster designs of *stile Liberty*, the Italian art nouveau period.

The design for this grapeseed oil for chef Jean-Georges Vongerichten combines a California and French sensibility—a West Coast color palette against a Provençal background motif.

The logo for Cathy B. Graham, an artist,
illustrator, floral arranger, and entertainer, was
inspired by her unique watercolor style.

Nº 19 ✦ 2014

Claudette, a light-filled restaurant on Fifth Avenue,
focuses on Provençal cuisine with North African influences.
The wrought-iron sign exudes the South of France.

The Housatonic River in Dalton, Massachusetts, home of the
eight-generation Crane & Co. paper mill, was the inspiration for
this monogram's natural flow of nesting Cs and ampersand.

CRAWFORD DOYLE
BOOKSELLERS

№ 21 ✦ 1997

Crawford Doyle Booksellers is an independent neighborhood bookstore on the Upper East Side of Manhattan. The letterpressed business card reflects the shop's timeless style.

For a Manhattan brasserie, what says *deluxe* better
than a classic two-toned French art deco typographic
treatment, in muted shades of lilac and mint?

№ 23 ✦ 2000

Ecco is an independent imprint of New York–based publisher
HarperCollins. The bold but distinctive letterforms of the
logo are effective when stamped on the spines of books.

ESPACE

BON APPETIT

Taking cues from a French sign painter's manual from the 1930s, the logo for this lively Union Square bistro was designed to look like a quintessential Parisian enamel sign.

№ 25 ✦ 2012

The graphics for Filaga, a Sicilian wood-fired
pizzeria in Manhattan's Chelsea Market, reference
early medieval Italian ceramic tile work.

No 26 ✦ 2013

Made with organic milk and state-of-the-art Italian
equipment, this gelato is crafted in Maine using traditional
techniques and the highest-quality ingredients.

The Giobatta logo was created in our studio kitchen, where we
boiled bucatini, spaghetti, and linguine to find the most suitable
for a script iteration. (Bucatini was the winner.)

LIMITED WARRANTY *to* CONSUMERS

· GOOD ·
HOUSEKEEPING

REPLACEMENT *or* REFUND *if* DEFECTIVE

Since ★ 1909

Nº 28 ✦ 2008

For the 100th anniversary of the Good Housekeeping Seal of
Approval, this redesign reflects the trust and reassurance of the
venerable warranty, exuding timeliness through restrained elegance.

Vintage neon signage inspired the type
treatment for the logo of this Houston
honky-tonk, Goodnight Charlie's.

Nº 30 ✦ 2001

Hanky Panky is an internationally recognized designer of women's intimate apparel. The company sells their celebrated lace thongs around the globe—at the rate of one per second.

the Harrison

355 GREENWICH ST.

AT HARRISON ST.

NEW YORK, NY

1 0 0 1 3

Ⓗ

Nº 31 ◆ 2001

The Harrison sounded like the name of a 1930s-style hotel.
The logo was created to resemble a vintage letterhead,
adapting a hand-lettered script from the period.

HONOLULU COFFEE CO

The logo for this artisan coffee roasting company evokes the lush and romantic Hawaiian travel posters from the 1930s. Since many customers cannot read English, the image needed to tell the story.

NO 33 ✦ 1989

The publishing division of Disney was named after the
location of the original studios on Hyperion Avenue
in Burbank. Hyperion is also a type of daylily.

Referencing Italian typographic design from
the early part of the 20th century, the labels
for Il Conte are virtual mini posters.

Il Mulino

—— NEW YORK ——

№ 35 ✦ 2004

This destination Italian restaurant in Greenwich Village
required a logo makeover before we embarked on the
package design for a line of signature pasta sauces.

Ilux imports fine intimate apparel from Italy. A woven
label sets it apart from the competition and creates a
memorable brand with high-quality workmanship.

The Inutilious Retailer

Nº 37 ✦ 2015

The Inutilious Retailer, on the Lower East Side, stocks over 1,000 Victorian wood blocks in the workshop in the back of the store, where you are invited to print your own clothing.

TRATTORIA ITALIENNE

№ 38 ✦ 2018

The logo for this Italian/French Provençal restaurant in
NoMad draws influence from art nouveau typography
and color palettes from both Italy and France.

Juliana's PIZZA

Nº 39 ✦ 2009

Juliana's, the celebrated pizzeria created by the
founders of Grimaldi's, is situated in Grimaldi's
original location in Dumbo, Brooklyn.

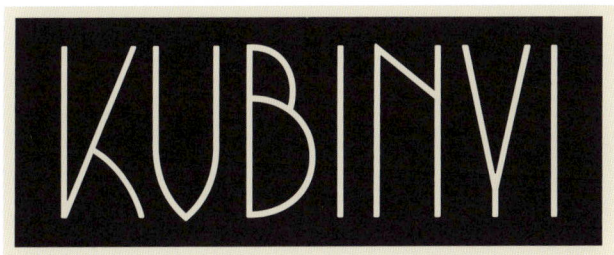

KUBINYI

Nº 40 ✦ 1986

The logo for fashion designer
Moisha Kubinyi references her
affinity for thirties-style couture.

L'Arte del GELATO™

Tradizione Siciliana

Nº 41 ✦ 2009

This sublime artisan Sicilian gelato is made every day in the
Chelsea Market, from fresh, seasonal ingredients. Italian
package designs from the 1930s informed the logo.

RESTAURANT
L'OSTAL

Nº 42 ✦ 2021

With Restaurant L'Ostal, chef Jared Sippel
(formerly of Trattoria Italienne) brings the best
of Provençal cuisine to Darien, Connecticut.

LA VARA

Comida Casera

La Vara offers Sephardic cuisine. The logo suggests
the tin ceiling of this landmarked Brooklyn space,
as well as a tile design motif used in the restaurant.

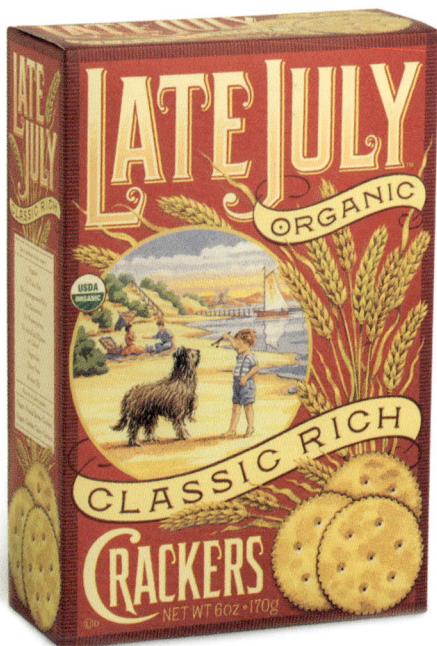

Vintage cracker graphics influenced the design
of the Late July packaging. All type on the front panel
of the box is hand-lettered, including the net weight.

Designed as a classic French enamel sign from the 1930s,
the logo for Le Monde, an uptown Manhattan brasserie, weds
vintage dimensional letterforms to a contemporary visual aesthetic.

The Magnolia Company

No 46 ✦ 2022

Over 20 years ago, The Magnolia Company started
making beautiful handcrafted wreaths. We recently had the
opportunity to create a more distinctive brand for the company.

MANHATTAN FRUITIER

Nº 47 ✦ 1998

The logo makeover for Manhattan Fruitier underscores
the graceful simplicity of this highly regarded purveyor of fruit
baskets that are reminiscent of Dutch still-life paintings.

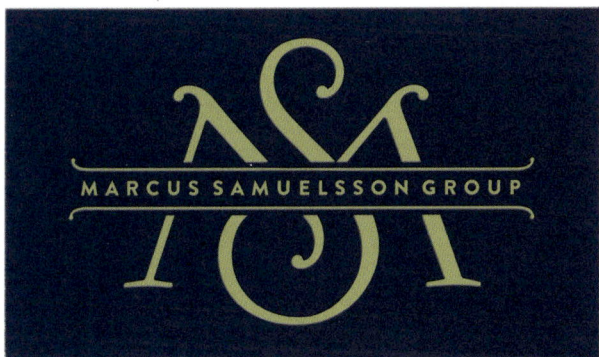

MARCUS SAMUELSSON GROUP

This logo was designed for the New York
City–based food media company of revered chef
Marcus Samuelsson, also the owner of Ambessa teas.

MARITIME

1251 AVENUE OF THE AMERICAS

NYC 10020 • TEL 212 354 1717

This deco-themed seafood restaurant called
for a unique logo, both bold and elegant,
containing four strategically placed red dots.

What better inspiration for a West Side French restaurant
than a classic Parisian neon script bistro sign? This logo was
fabricated into a replica of an early 20th-century marquee.

The Mermaid Inn is an East Village seafood shack. When
sibling restaurant Mermaid Oyster Bar followed, the iconic ladyfish
was flipped, and a pearl choker was added around her neck.

MÉTRAZUR

GRAND CENTRAL TERMINAL

EAST BALCONY

NYC
TEL
212
687
4600

Nº 52 ✦ 1993

Named after a train line along the French Riviera, this restaurant on the balcony of Grand Central Terminal required a special business card, letterpressed to resemble a luggage tag.

Metro Grill
NEW YORK

Nº 53 ✦ 1997

Located in the Garment District of New York, Metro Grill
features a logo made into an actual stitched clothing label, which
is used on the menus, servers' shirts, and chefs' baseball caps.

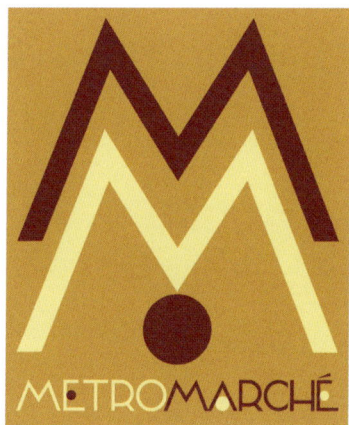

METROMARCHÉ

Nº 54 ✦ 2006

A French bistro is unlikely to find itself in
Manhattan's Port Authority Terminal, but this
deco-styled logo helped make the transition.

This *brasserie française* in Manhattan's Flatiron
District featured a map of the neighborhood on
the back of the business card, all written in French.

The packaging for Mezzetta's 75-year-old family business was in dire need of an overhaul. A new logo, label design, and custom bottle made all the difference for this respected brand.

MONZÙ

142 MERCER ST

NYC 10012

212 343

0333

Designed in a triangular shape to refer to the island of Sicily, this logo was made into a die-cut, letterpress-printed business card that was also tipped onto colored paper stock for the menus.

The logo for this Vietnamese restaurant located
in the food court at Grand Central Terminal was
made from chopsticks, as was the dimensional sign.

This restaurant logo pays tribute to New York
City's iconic mosaic subway tiles, and convinced many
customers of the existence of a 92nd Street stop.

№ 60 ✦ 2018

Officina 1397 is the restaurant group for
celebrated chefs Rita Sodi and Jody Williams,
owners of Via Carota and Pisellino.

A custom-printed cork with a well-placed slit
made the perfect check presenter for this classic Italian
wine bar at the Borgata Hotel in Atlantic City.

The Italian word for peace, *pace* was not easy for the dining
public to pronounce correctly. A small sticker was designed
to close the matchbox, with the translation in parentheses.

№ 63 ✦ 2010

A custom script evokes the lost art of correspondence for this logo makeover for Paperless Post, an online resource for beautifully personalized stationery.

№ 64 ✦ 2007

A logo for a dentist shouldn't have to look ordinary.
The identity for Paul Tanners, a Madison Avenue
prosthodontist, is as unique and distinctive as his practice.

Pearl

O Y S T E R · B A R

Nº 65 ✦ 2012

Pearl Oyster Bar introduced the lobster-roll craze to
Manhattan in the 1990s, without a logo. Fifteen years later,
we were asked to give Pearl the graphic identity it deserved.

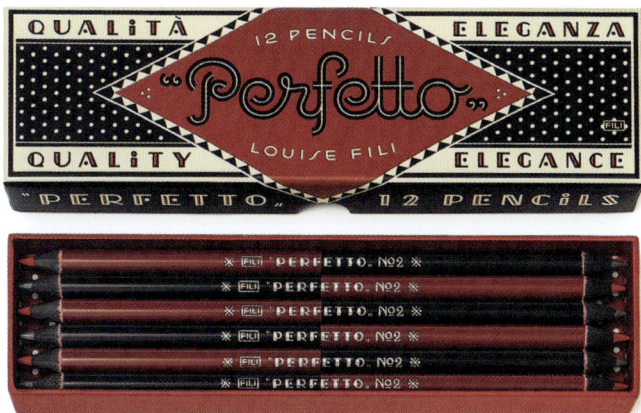

Vintage Italian pencil boxes inspired
a set of double-sided, two-tone pencils,
using a classic 1930s cursive.

picholine

Picholine, a type of French olive, was a challenging word
for people to spell, pronounce, and remember. The logo
is a visual memory aid to reinforce the meaning of the word.

Nº 68 ✦ 2000

This deco-themed logo for a French restaurant in
the heart of Manhattan's Theater District suggests the
spirited and eccentric Pigalle neighborhood in Paris.

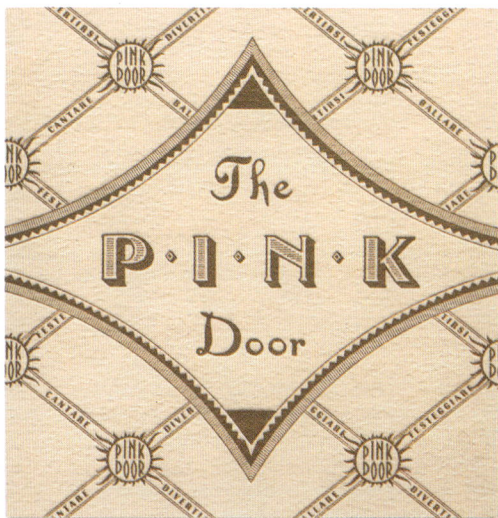

The PINK Door

The design of the Pink Door logo signals the eclectic character of this vibrant Italian eatery in Seattle. The pattern and typography are reminiscent of 1930s *pasticceria* papers from Italy.

52 GROVE ST · NYC

Pisellino

· BAR ·

№ 70 ✦ 2019

Located across the street from its sister
restaurant, Via Carota, Pisellino will transport
you into a bar in Rome, Florence, or Venice.

Post 390 is a casual and fine-dining restaurant
in Boston's Back Bay neighborhood, built
on the site of a former post office.

Poulet Sans Tête serves humanely raised rotisserie chickens in Greenwich Village. Referencing French illuminated signs, the logo was made into a blinking neon sign of its own.

A French deco typographic treatment with intersecting
Xs created a memorable logo for Prix Fixe, a unique
concept restaurant in Manhattan's Flatiron District.

A debossed, embossed, and foil-stamped label embodies tactile elegance for this ultra-premium Cabernet Sauvignon from the Napa Valley.

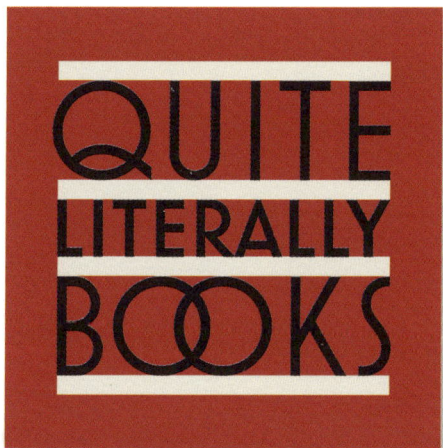

This logo for a female-owned publishing company that
reissues novels written by unknown women authors
transforms the type into books sitting on a shelf.

RIVE GAUCHE

Nº 76 ✦ 1999

Too many partners could not decide on a name for this restaurant—
only that it would be a Parisian locale. This street sign artwork was
at the ready, waiting for the two words to be dropped in.

roseville

Nº 77 ✦ 2008

Located in the historic Roseville neighborhood
of San Diego, this restaurant called for a
graceful Victorian type treatment.

Royale Montaine

PAVILLON D'ORANGE

ORANGE LIQUEUR
with DELICATE
COGNAC

750ML · 40% ALC./VOL.

№ 78 ✦ 2022

The label for Royale Montaine, an orange
liqueur, incorporates a classic upright French
script alongside a vintage-inspired illustration.

RUBIROSA

EXTRA VIRGIN
OLIVE OIL

Nº 79 ✦ 2022

Rubirosa, the Italian American family-owned Manhattan
restaurant and pizzeria, introduced their first product line:
Marinara Sauce, Vodka Sauce, and Extra Virgin Olive Oil.

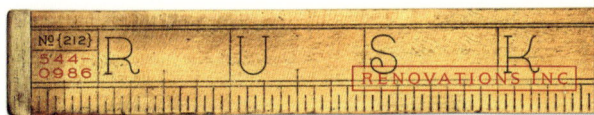

An antique ruler was turned into a logo for the high-quality contracting team of Rusk Renovations, who pride themselves on skilled craftsmanship using time-honored techniques.

BARTLETT
SPIRITS · OF · MAINE · DISTILLERY

ESTᴰ · 1983

RUSTICATOR RUM

SMALL · BATCH

DISTILLED
IN MAINE

750 ML · 45% ALC/VOL

№ 81 ◆ 2013

Rusticator Rum is made with organic molasses from
South America. The name suggests late 19th-century city
dwellers who escaped to Maine in search of cooler climes.

A careful typographic overhaul, after 25
years, gave Sarabeth's packages a look that
measures up to her exemplary reputation.

THE SCREENING ROOM
restaurant and cinema

Nº 83 ✦ 1998

Plaster letters once used for making home movie
titles were combined with photomontaged images
for this restaurant and cinema with a 1940s theme.

Sfida, which means *challenge* in Italian, was an aptly
named wine, since an enormous amount of copy needed
to fit onto a label of a very specific size and shape.

The Italian term for sheets of handmade pasta, Sfoglia is a
restaurant with locations in both Nantucket and Manhattan.
The two islands are represented by two mermaids.

STONEWOOD · FARM

MILLBROOK · NEW YORK

№ 86 ✦ 2014

Stonewood Farm is a small-scale, diversified
vegetable and flower farm using organic
practices in New York's Hudson Valley.

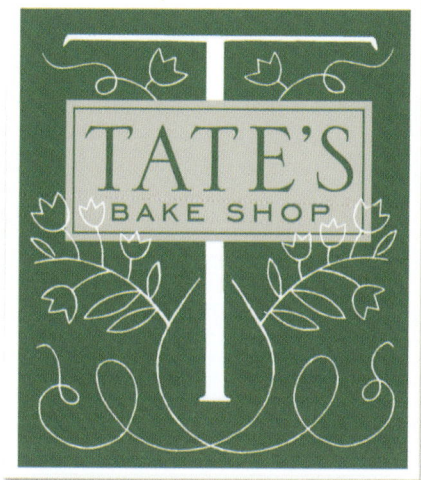

TATE'S
BAKE SHOP

Tate's top-rated chocolate-chip cookies (and cakes, pies, brownies, and blondies) are impossible to resist. Victorian-era illuminated letterforms inspired the logotype and packaging.

Nº 88 ✦ 2008

For Terrazzo Prosecco, the goal was to make the
type look effervescent; the result was a hand-drawn
script and a border printed in subtle metallic colors.

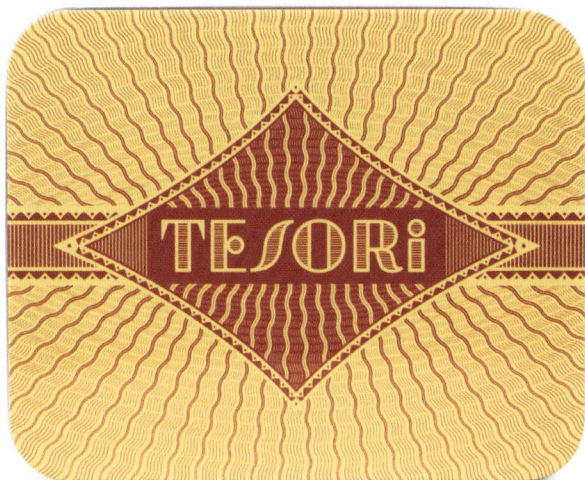

Whether an elegant cache for colored pencils, a repository for
recipes, or a special spot for family photographs, these nesting tins
("treasures" in Italian) bring order and delight to any desktop.

Creating a mark for Tiffany posed a challenge: to design
a monogram that could be used small enough for the winder
of a man's watch, or large enough for a construction shed.

Nº 91 ✦ 2009

Tratturi, from the Salento region of Italy (the heel of the boot), uses a pattern created to evoke the *trulli*, or cone-shaped huts, that are emblematic of the region.

ELEGANZA · COLORATA

12 PENCILS

Tutti Frutti

LOUISE FILI

COLORFUL · ELEGANCE

12 PENCILS · 6 · COLORS

Nº 92 ✦ 2015

A follow-up to the black-and-red double-sided Perfetto
pencils, Tutti Frutti colored pencils come in six different
hues, and will bring out everyone's inner Caravaggio.

Txikito is an intimate Chelsea restaurant featuring Basque cuisine. The logo is a nod to wrought-iron script signage found in this region of Spain.

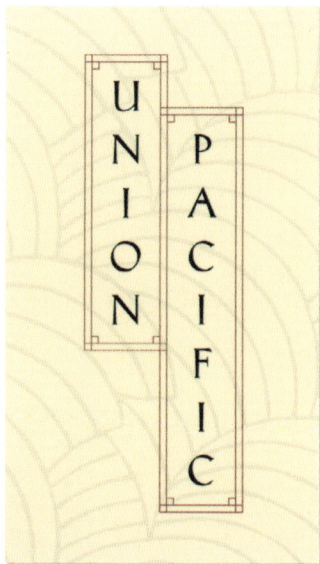

A restaurant near Union Square (sort of) with neo-Asian
cuisine had nothing to do with the railroad. Vertically stacked
type was essential in order to communicate this message.

VANDENBERG
THE TOWNHOUSE
EXPERTS

Nº 95 ✦ 2005

A classic architectural detail was the perfect way to
represent this real estate company known for its expertise
in buying and selling unique Manhattan townhouses.

VIA CAROTA

51 GROVE STREET

N · Y · C

Nº 96 ✦ 2015

Via Carota, a West Village gastroteca, is named after a
street in the Tuscan town of Bagno a Ripoli. The typography
of early 20th-century Italian posters informed the logo.

A Victorian-themed monogram was the ideal way to represent Kent Wang, a self-described "modern haberdasher," known for his signature hand-sewn silk pocket square.

№ 98 ✦ 2012

Xelda is a unique accessories
line for a fashion designer who
references the art deco period.

Yes We Can is a chef's collective organized just
after the 2008 presidential campaign in an attempt
to change the way Americans think about food.

Elaine from *Seinfeld* introduced Zelda's exquisite 1930s-inspired jackets to a wider audience. The logo pays tribute to French fashion illustration from the deco period.

MY SINCERE THANKS TO THE CLIENTS FOR WHOM THESE IDENTITIES WERE CREATED: MARCUS SAMUELSSON, NOAH Marshall-Rashid, Terrance Brennan, Richard Gere and Carey Lowell, Alisa Barry, Harold Kyle, Roberto and Monica Bellissimo, Rachel Greenspan and Brendan Smith, Robert Cole, Whendi and Phil Grad, Edwina Von Gal, Bonnie Shershow, Peter Matt, Douglas Polaner and Tina Fischer, Jean-Georges Vongerichten, Cathy B. Graham, Carlos Suarez, Judy Crawford and John Doyle, Dan Halpern, Andrew Silverman, Francesco Realmuto, Joshua Davis, Michele Platt and Francesco Buitoni, Gale Epstein and Lida Orzeck, Danny Abrams, Jimmy Bradley, Adrian Wilson, Jared Sippel and Lindsey Kilmurray, Matthew Grogan, Moisha Blechman, Alex Raij and Eder Montero, Nicole Dawes, Simon Oren, Julie and Matt Roth, Jehv Gold, Michael and Karen Miele, Jeff Mezzetta, Jean Goutal, Ken Aretsky, James and Alexa Hirschfeld, Rebecca Charles, Jackie Roberts, Laurence Edelman and Micheline Gaulin, Jessica and Natan Bibliowitz, John Cooper, Mary Kocy and John Rusk, Bob and Kathe Bartlett, Sarabeth and Bill Levine, Ron Suhanosky, Ken Holzberg and Tom Kopfensteiner, Paul Tanners, dds, Kathleen King, Rocco DiSpirito, Jane Ordway, Jody Williams and Rita Sodi, Bremond Berry MacDougall and Lisa Endo Cooper, Kent Wang, and Renee Shaw.

Most importantly, thank you to the talented designers who have worked at Louise Fili Ltd to help bring these designs to life: Christian Adamsky, Andy Anzollitto, Rebecca Bartlett, Lee Bearson, Jennifer Blanco, Mary Jane Callister, Phaedra Charles, Courtney Eckersley, Andy Evans, Raphael Geroni, Lesley Hathaway, Jessica Hische, Tonya Hudson, Leah Lococo, Nicholas Misani, John Passafiume, Abbey Prokell, Chad Roberts, Matthew Smith, Dana Tanamachi, Kelly Thorn, and Michelle Willems. Also to the illustrators who have contributed their artistry: Graham Evernden, Mirko Ilić, Gary Kelley, Melanie Parks, Anthony Russo, Dugald Stermer, and Christopher Wormell.

I am indebted to David Rhodes, Anthony Rhodes, Richard Wilde, Francis Di Tommaso, and Gail Anderson at School of Visual Arts for the opportunity to teach at the college and to be part of the Masters Series award and exhibition, from which this book originated.

A heartfelt thank you to Jennifer Thompson and Paul Wagner at Princeton Architectural Press.

As always, love and gratitude to my family, Steven and Nicolas Heller, for their endless support.